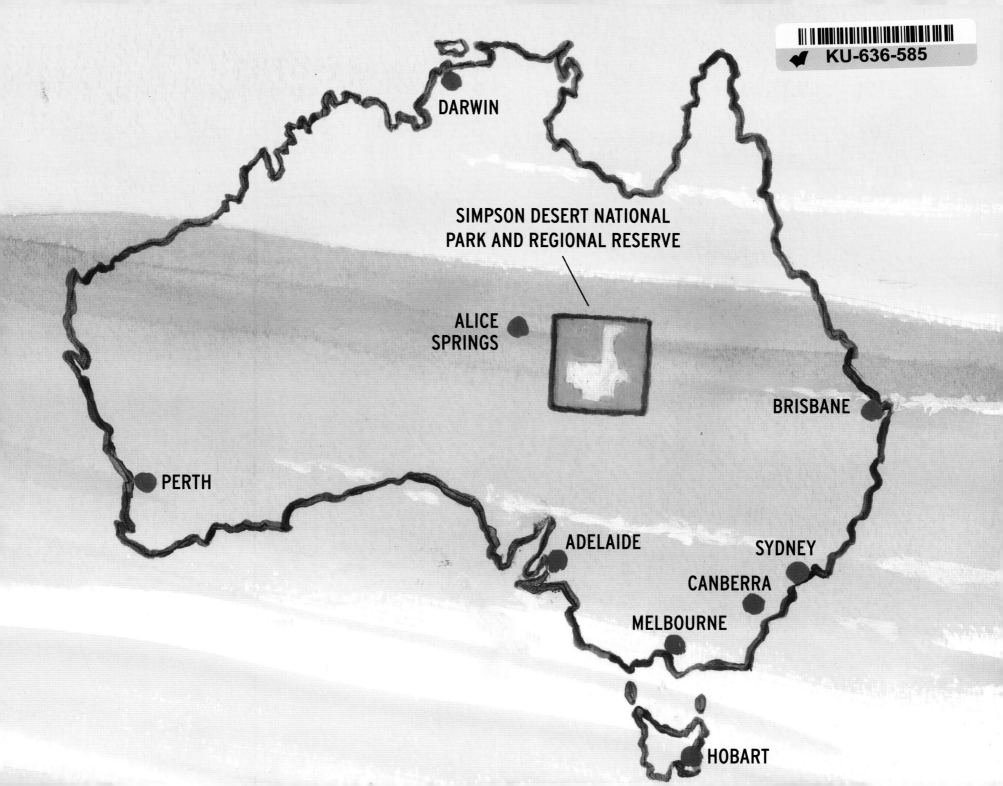

DARWIN

SIMPSON DESERT NATIONAL
PARK AND REGIONAL RESERVE

ALICE
SPRINGS

BRISBANE

PERTH

ADELAIDE

SYDNEY

CANBERRA

MELBOURNE

HOBART

To Chris, Bobby, Aaron, Nik, Anke, and Tony and the wonderful team of scientists and volunteers from the April 2010 Simpson Desert trip. Cheers to twenty years of research —D. M.

May children read and learn of the different places in the world — J. V. Z.

Published 2013 by A & C Black, am imprint of Bloomsbury Publishing Plc
50 Bedford Square, London, WC1B 3DP
www.bloomsbury.com

First published in the United States of America in 2012 by Walker Publishing Company, Inc.

ISBN 978-1-4081-9029-6

Text copyright © 2012 Debbie S. Miller
Illustration copyright © 2012 Jon Van Zyle

This art was created with acrylic on 300-lb coldpress water colour paper

Book design by Nicole Gastonguay

A CIP record for this book is available from the British Library.

This book is produced using paper that is made from wood grown in managed, sustainable forests. It is natural, renewable and recyclable. The logging and manufacturing processes conform to the environmental regulations of the country of origin.

Printed in China by South China Printing Company

10 9 8 7 6 5 4 3 2 1

ACKNOWLEDGMENTS

A very special thanks to Chris Dickman at the University of Sydney's Institute of Wildlife Research for inviting me to be a volunteer on one of their scientific research trips to the Simpson Desert. Camping in the desert allowed me to study the fascinating animals that are well adapted to this hot, dry environment. Thanks to Bush Heritage, a conservation organization that manages reserves within the Simpson Desert and supports scientific research. I'm also grateful to the Alaska State Council on the Arts for a grant that helped cover some of the travel expenses to Australia.

In the Simpson Desert there were many biologists and scientists who answered questions about desert life and who reviewed and critiqued my manuscript. Their knowledge and field experience enabled me to write this book. Many thanks to: Anke Frank, Niki Hill, Bobby Tamayo, Aaron Greenville, Tony Popic, Max Tischler, and Adam Kerezsy. Last, a heartfelt thanks to Richard Nelson, who introduced me to Australia and the wonderful group of people who study desert ecology and who also shared his great animal sound recordings so that children can listen to the voices of the desert world.

EAST RIDING
OF YORKSHIRE COUNCIL
Schools Library Service
PROJECT
February 2013

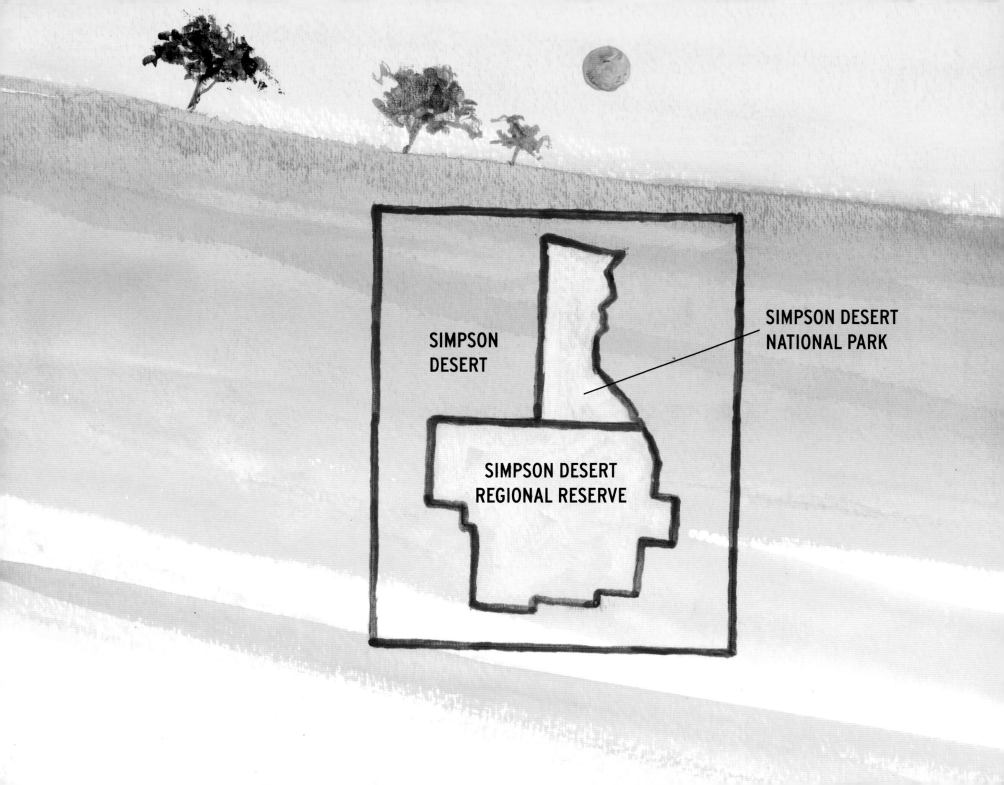

Survival at 40°C Above

Debbie S. Miller

ILLUSTRATED BY Jon Van Zyle

A & C BLACK
AN IMPRINT OF BLOOMSBURY
LONDON   NEW DELHI   NEW YORK   SYDNEY

As the night sky melts away, the Simpson Desert horizon glows like a campfire. Creaking voices of crickets grow faint. The dawn air is dry and warm when the chiming wedgebill sings its five note song, "Time to get up now . . . time to get up now."

A brilliant sun peeks above the longest parallel sand dunes in the world. As soft as powder,

the stunning sand is the colour of a red brick. In early days, people called this arid land the "Great Ribbed Desert" because of the long, wind shaped dunes that twist and turn across Australia for hundreds of miles (kilometres). This vast, rippled desert bakes beneath a dome of a forever blue sky.

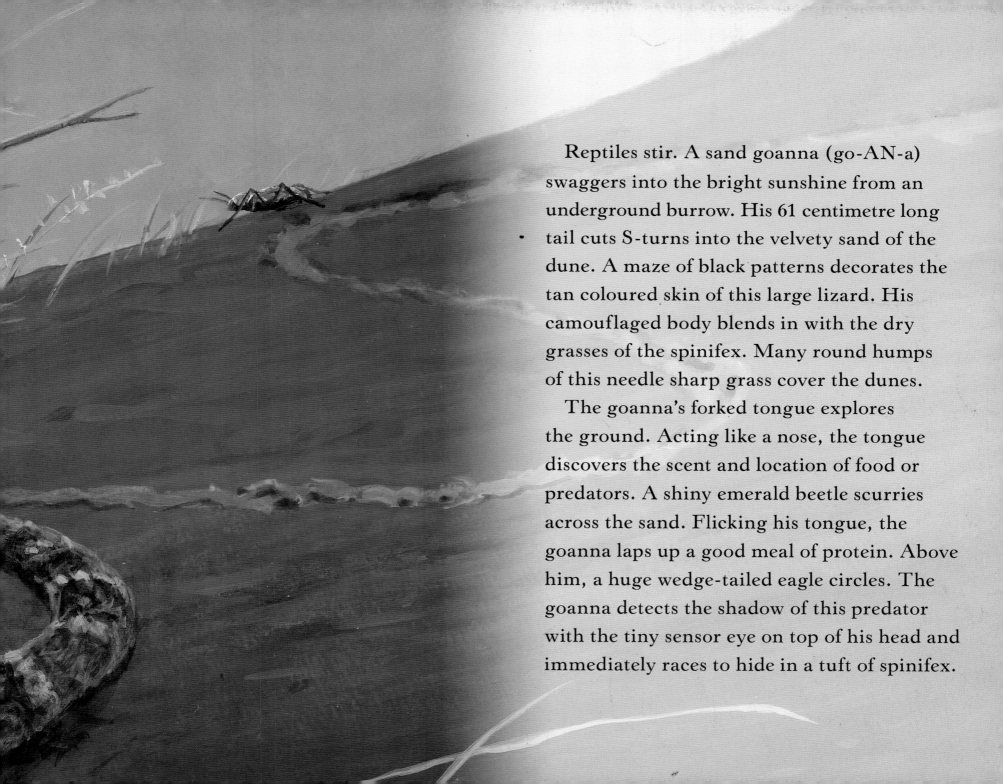

Reptiles stir. A sand goanna (go-AN-a) swaggers into the bright sunshine from an underground burrow. His 61 centimetre long tail cuts S-turns into the velvety sand of the dune. A maze of black patterns decorates the tan coloured skin of this large lizard. His camouflaged body blends in with the dry grasses of the spinifex. Many round humps of this needle sharp grass cover the dunes.

The goanna's forked tongue explores the ground. Acting like a nose, the tongue discovers the scent and location of food or predators. A shiny emerald beetle scurries across the sand. Flicking his tongue, the goanna laps up a good meal of protein. Above him, a huge wedge-tailed eagle circles. The goanna detects the shadow of this predator with the tiny sensor eye on top of his head and immediately races to hide in a tuft of spinifex.

By noon the sand is blistering hot beneath a cloudless sky. The temperature rises to more than 40 degrees Celsius. For seven years the desert has faced a great drought, with only an occasional sprinkling of rain. Seeds lie dormant, lacking enough moisture to sprout. During this scorching time, the goanna moves to a grove of gidgee trees. With barbed claws, he climbs a tree seeking shade and a breeze. Other reptiles tunnel beneath the sand to find cooler ground.

Near the goanna, a mob of red kangaroos rests in the shade of the trees. Some of the kangaroos lick their arms and paws to cool themselves. When a breeze drifts through the open woodland, moisture evaporates from their fur, which lowers their body temperature. Kangaroos, which are the world's largest marsupial also have special hair that helps reflect sun rays. Each shiny strand acts like a tiny mirror.

In the afternoon, a blustery wind signals a change in the weather. Puffy clouds run across the sky with sheets of rain streaming beneath them. These misty curtains of rain, known as virga, evaporate before reaching the ground due to rising heat. The scattered clouds bring cooler temperatures and a patchwork of shade to the red sand.

At last, a few drops reach the ground, followed by a light drizzle. Suddenly, as though someone turned on a tap, the light drizzle changes to pouring rain. Each drop finds a home on a grain of sand, a leathery leaf, or the fur of a kangaroo. Withered roots welcome the rain like a dry kitchen sponge. Now the desert is really wet!

Parched creek beds turn into bubbling streams, meandering across the desert. Dry claypans, wrinkled with cracks, turn into swamps. Patient fairy shrimp eggs hatch after baking in the dry clay for seven long years. Triops erupt from this new source of life. These minnow like crustaceans grow domed shells that look like tiny horseshoe crabs. Rainbowfish squiggle up the meandering creeks, migrating to new ponds.

Glunk . . . glunk . . . glunk. It sounds like someone is playing a distant bongo. Filling her throat pouch with air, a female emu makes a drumming sound as she strides across the open woodland. She smells water.

This huge, flightless bird looks like a grass hut walking on scaly stilts. Like an ostrich, her round body is covered with feathers. Well adapted to the heat, her loose, open feathers allow air to pass through them. They shade and cool her body. As she moves towards the distant water, her giant three toed feet support her in the soft sand.

While emus saunter across the dunes, herons, pelicans, and other waterbirds fly overhead. Sensing the distant rain, these birds fly hundreds of miles from the coast to feast on the explosion of life in the desert swamps. It is a mystery how these birds sense the rain, sometimes from 1,000 miles away.

Wearing a spiny coat of armour, a thorny devil crawls slowly from his burrow. Only 20 cm long, this unique lizard looks like a miniature ankylosaurus dinosaur. The top of his body is completely covered with thorny spikes, protecting him from predators. Soon he discovers a trail of tiny black ants, his only food source. Thrusting out his sticky tongue, he devours the ants one by one. The thorny devil can eat as many as 3,000 ants in one day.

Standing in a patch of wet sand, the thorny devil reveals his drinking secret. Through capillary action, this lizard can drink this water from his feet. The water moves upward along narrow grooves on the skin's surface from his toes, up his legs, to the corners of his mouth, similar to the way a plant drinks water from its roots.

A blue-tailed skink searches for a bright patch of sunshine. Darting across the sand, this striped lizard discovers a perfect spot to bask in the sunlight that also offers a good lookout for possible predators. As the skink warms himself, a venomous western brown snake is slithering towards him.

The well camouflaged snake draws closer, curving through the grasses. Suddenly, the skink hears a rustling sound. Immediately he begins waving his blue tail. It looks like the lizard is performing a hula dance. Attracted by the movement, the snake's head races forward. Her gaping mouth tries to bite the dancing tail. Instantly, the end of the lizard's tail breaks off, and the skink dashes away into the safety of the spinifex. The skink will grow a new tail, a special adaptation for survival. Some lizards lose and regrow their tails several times during their lives.

As the sun slips below the horizon, the peach coloured sky deepens to the shade of strawberries. The dunes begin to cool. An Australian raven closes the day with his moaning call: *Ah . . . Ah . . . Ahhhhhhhhhh.* On cue, the voices of crickets loudly fill the air like thousands of castanets.

Nocturnal animals grow restless in their burrows. A brush-tailed mulgara (mul-GAR-uh) cautiously peeks out of an exit hole, sniffing the air. She smells the faint scent of a dingo, but not to worry – the wild dog's tracks are several days old.

The mulgara has sensitive black eyes designed for night vision. In the soft moon-light this predator detects a sandy inland mouse. The quick mulgara scampers along the trail of tiny round footprints. Pounce! She snatches the mouse as he feeds on some dried seeds. No longer hungry, the mulgara returns to her burrow. This hamster size marsupial plays an important role in controlling rodents and keeping the diversity of desert life in balance.

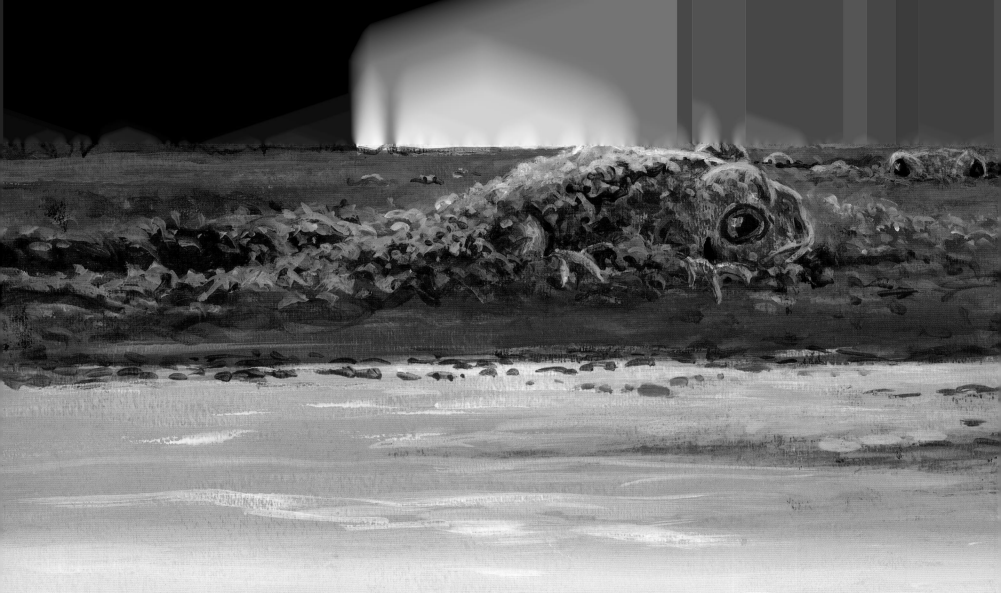

Pockets of sand begin to move. Brown heads speckled with orange spots break through the surface of the sand. After many dormant months of rest, known as estivation, desert spadefoot frogs explode from the ground. Near midnight, hundreds of these amphibians begin croaking for their mates near the edge of a pond.

The chorus of frogs attracts other animals. White wings suddenly flash through the darkness. A spotted nightjar cuts swiftly through the air. He

dives at a frog, attempting to snatch it from the ground. The warty frog quickly protects itself by secreting a milky liquid from it's poison glands through the skin of it's neck. When the nightjar bites the frog, this sticky white goo acts like glue.

The goo cements the mouth of the nightjar so it can't eat the frog. It's a superglue frog!

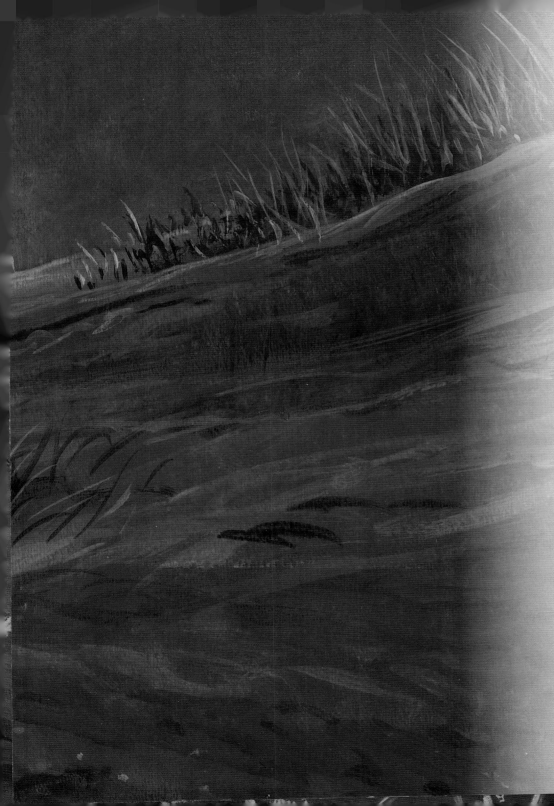

A ningaui (nin-GOW-ee) stirs. She feels the cool night air and leaves her underground home. This thumb size creature is one of the smallest marsupials and weighs as little as six paper clips. Dashing between the spinifex, her tiny cone shaped head and flattened ears allow her to squeeze through thick clumps of grasses. As she hunts for beetles and spiders, the sound of a running animal startles her. She spots the fleeting shadow of a doglike creature.

The panting dingo is chasing a large feral house cat. Sand flying, the sleek cat races through the obstacle course of spinifex. While the dingo is a larger animal, the wild cat is quick and nimble. He slips away, springing over bushes, escaping over the crest of the dune. The hidden ningaui is lucky. Feral cats are fierce predators, feeding on many small marsupials and reptiles. The dingo helps control cats and other feral animals so that native species, such as ningaui and mulgara, can survive.

At dawn, red kangaroos feed on fresh green shoots. They are most active during dusk and dawn when the temperatures are cooler. Creatures that like the twilight are crepuscular animals.

As one mother kangaroo grazes, her joey (baby kangaroo) listens to a pair of Australian magpies singing their beautiful duet. Joining the magpies is a loud chorus of cooing frogs and creaking crickets.

Beyond the kangaroos a lone camel plods over the dune, leaving plate size tracks in the sand. This one humped dromedary camel can live for months without water, yet he smells the rain fed swamp and marches toward it. Like other desert animals and plants, the camel will thrive on the gift of rain.

The desert is a sea of green and red in the early morning light. Like cresting waves, the dunes rise and fall above green swales and newly formed swamps. The endless ridges of red sand create a land similar to the wavy texture of corduroy.

The emus discover a swamp after traveling many miles. They kneel in the shallow water, splashing themselves with their stubby wings. Surrounding them are white-necked herons, avocets, and pink-eared ducks. These birds are feasting on the fairy shrimp, triops, and other aquatic invertebrates. The long seven year drought is over. For a short time life will flourish in this vast and beautiful land of red.

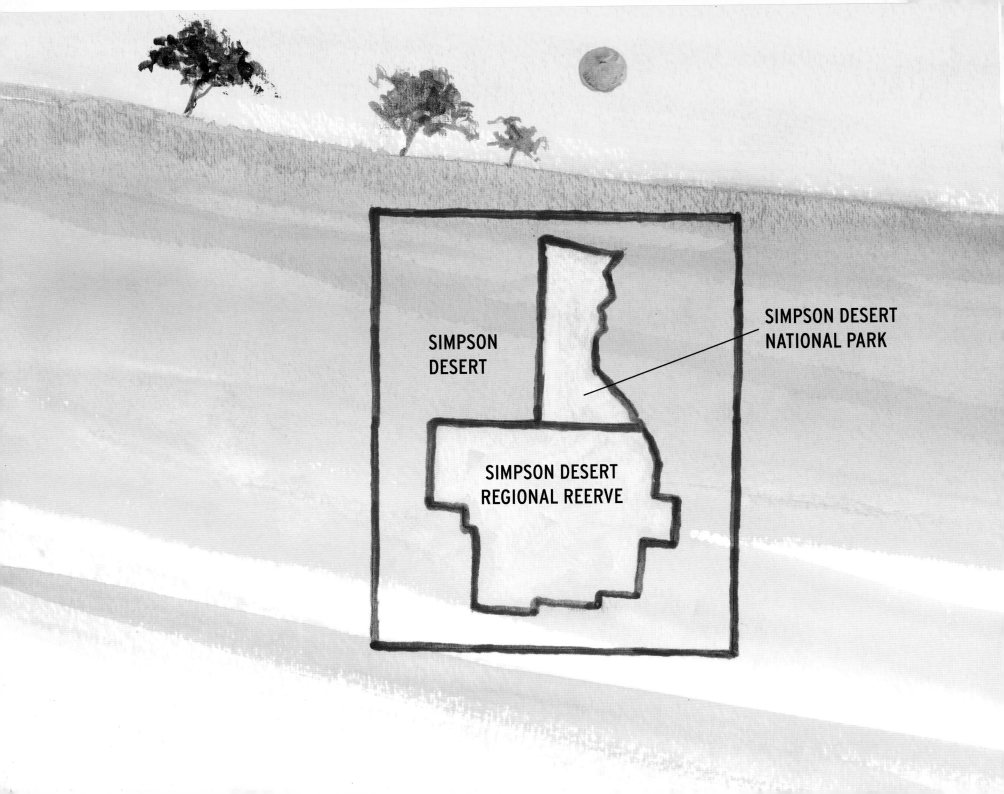

SIMPSON
DESERT

SIMPSON DESERT
NATIONAL PARK

SIMPSON DESERT
REGIONAL REERVE

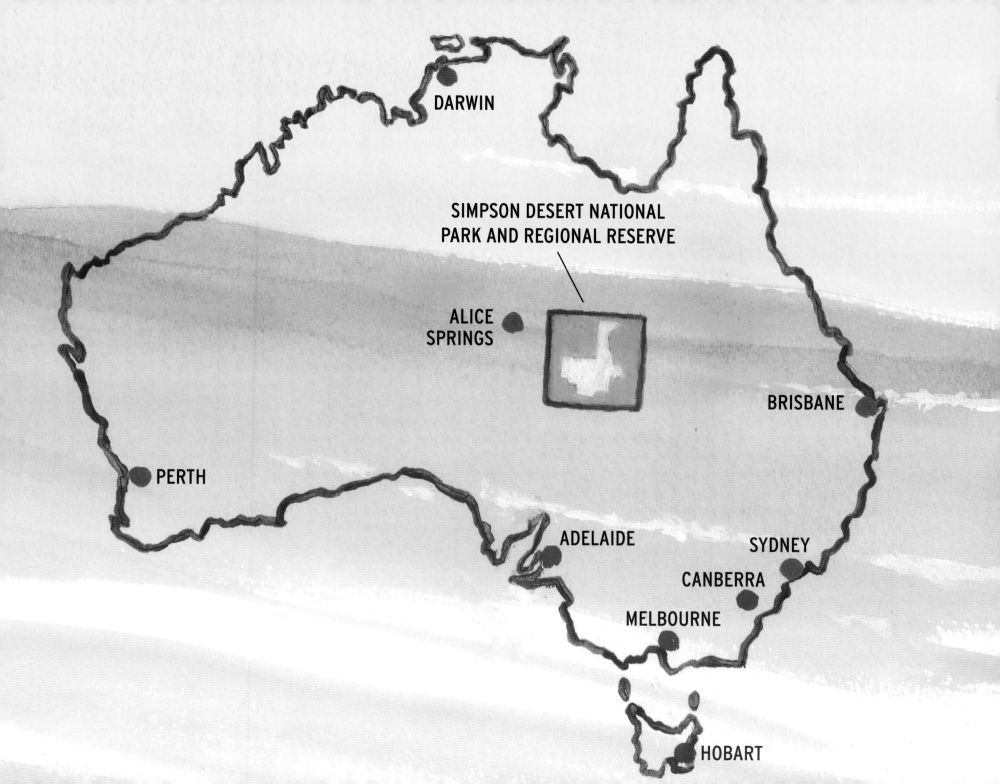

DARWIN

SIMPSON DESERT NATIONAL
PARK AND REGIONAL RESERVE

ALICE
SPRINGS

BRISBANE

PERTH

ADELAIDE

SYDNEY

CANBERRA

MELBOURNE

HOBART

DEBBIE S. MILLER is the author of *Survival at 40 Below* and *Arctic Nights, Arctic Lights*, both of which were chosen as Outstanding Science Trade Books for Children by the National Science Teacher Association/CBC. Debbie lives with her family in Fairbanks, Alaska. www.debbiemilleralaska.com

JON VAN ZYLE has teamed up with Debbie S. Miller on nine Alaskan themed books, including *A Polar Bear Journey* and *The Great Serum Race*, which was chosen as a Notable Social Studies Trade Book for Young People by the National Council for Social Studies/CBC. Jon is also the official artist of the Iditarod Trail Sled Dog Race and lives with his wife and their Siberian huskies in Eagle River, Alaska. www.jonvanzyle.com